FIFTY
WILDFLOWERS
BEAR VALLEY
COLUSA COUNTY

D1176725

JOHN GAME & RICHARDS LYON

ACKNOWLEDGEMENTS

Cover Photograph by Bob Stephens
Title Page Photograph by Stephen W. Edwards
Map by Laura Lyon

BEAR VALLEY WILDFLOWERS

Bear Valley, in northern California's Colusa County, is home to one of the most spectacular wildflower displays in the world. Sweeping vistas of color cover several thousand acres each spring, evolving as the season progresses. The Bear Valley palette changes each year, influenced by both the intensity and the mixture of rain, heat, and sunlight.

In all, more than 400 different plants have been identified in the Valley and the surrounding ridges. We have chosen 50 of the Valley's most interesting or commonly seen flowers for this book. To aid in identification, flowers are arranged by color rather than by plant families. However, many additional species will be seen in Bear Valley beyond those mentioned in the limited scope of this book.

The American Land Conservancy is committed to preserving this small remnant of the once extensive wildflower displays that carpeted the Central Valley and the surrounding ranges.

We would like to thank the many people who have helped with this project. Special thanks to John Game, Richards Lyon and Laura Lyon for writing and editing this book, to Richards Lyon, John Game, Steve Edwards, and Jake Rugyt for providing their photographs, and to the California Native Plant Society for their ongoing support.

Generous contributions from The Strong Foundation for Environmental Values, the Resort Design Group, and Sunsweet Growers Inc. have underwritten this book's publication. Additional support was provided by Sierra Nevada Brewing Company, Inc., and the Yuba-Sutter Appeal-Democrat.

DEDICATION

This book is dedicated to the memory of George M. Clark (1938-1996). He was the president of the California Native Plant Society from 1995 to 1996. George was a self-taught botanist, a dedicated conservationist and beloved friend to all who knew him. George loved Bear Valley and the neighboring Walker Ridge and introduced their plants to hundreds of people through his field trips. On June 9, 1996 George died while exploring Walker Ridge for new plant populations. It was George's dream that Bear Valley would be preserved along with Walker Ridge to forever delight the eyes and refresh the souls of its visitors.

Eva Butler
CNPS

American Land Conservancy is dedicated to the preservation of land and water as enduring public resources, and to the protection and enhancement of our nation's natural, ecological, historical, and scenic heritage. Compelled by the urgent need to conserve intact our irreplaceable natural and wildland resources, ALC seeks to preserve the diversity of native plant, wildlife and aquatic communities, to guard and restore the natural integrity of ecosystems, and to expand opportunities for public recreation, education, and scientific research. ALC is committed to promoting a national land ethic to achieve responsible stewardship of our public lands and waters for the benefit of present and future generations.

American Land Conservancy
456 Montgomery Street, Suite 1450
San Francisco, CA 94104
415-403-3850
fax - 415-403-3856
e-mail - alc@econet.org

Richards Lyon

Stephen W. Edwards

WHITE HYACINTH
Triteleia hyacinthina
Family Lily

This grows in meadows, especially near the north end of Bear Valley, and is recognized by clusters of white flowers at the top of an upright stem. After flowering, it goes dormant in summer until the winter rains come. This is a common adaptation in plants that thrive in our climate of dry summers and wet winters. Similar species are found in other places with this climate, but California is especially rich in attractive wild bulbs of the Lily family.
Blooms April to May

LONG-RAYED BRODIAEA
Triteleia peduncularis
Family Lily

This plant can be seen in the northern meadows of Bear Valley. It is rather similar to White Hyacinth, but has much longer stalks supporting each flower in the cluster. It also grows in damper spots. Ithuriel's Spear is another relative, but this is easily distinguished by deep blue flowers instead of the whitish color of Long-Rayed Brodiaea.
Blooms April to May

Richards Lyon

Stephen W. Edwards

FREMONT'S ZYGADENE
Zigadenus fremontii
Family Lily

This plant has poisonous bulbs and is closely related to Death Camas (*Zigadenus venenosus*), which is also found in this area. Fremont's Zygadene occurs in large numbers west of Bear Valley Road just north of the largest Adobe Lily population. It has strap-shaped leaves near the base and tall stems with numerous flowers. The petals are white with pale yellow marks.
Blooms April

CALIFORNIA DWARF FLAX
Hesperolinon californicum
Family Flax

This small annual has branching upright stems and delicate white flowers. It grows in rocky areas influenced by serpentine soil in the south part of Bear Valley and on nearby Walker Ridge. At least a dozen other kinds of Dwarf Flax are known. Many of them are very rare and most are found only in California. This species is uncommon, but is known from several hilly regions in the north and center of the state.
Blooms May to June.

SNOWDROP BUSH
Styrax Officinalis
Family Storax

This is one of California's most beautiful native shrubs. The fragrant white flowers droop in clusters from the ends of the branchlets. They are offset by attractive light green leaves that are round to oval and hairy on the undersides. Snowdrop Bush grows in dry rocky areas and can be seen along the southern part of Bear Valley Road and on Walker Ridge. It is deciduous, so that only its gray bark is visible in winter.

Blooms May to June

WOOLLY MALACOTHRIX
Malacothrix floccifera
Family Sunflower

The leaves of this plant are in a rosette at the base, and the "Woolly" part of the name refers to the small patches of dense cobwebby hairs in the axils of the leaf lobes. It is common on open brushy slopes and along the road in the southern part of Bear Valley. Although it is a member of the sunflower family, the flower heads do not have a separate central "disk" like Goldfields or Tidy Tips.

Blooms April to May

John Game

John Game

MARIPOSA LILY

Calochortus luteus X superbus
Family Lily

Mariposa Lilies are among California's most beautiful wildflowers. At least three kinds are found in Bear Valley. Splendid Mariposa is pictured on page 51. Superb Mariposa and Yellow Mariposa occur and hybridize here, to give a great variety of colors. Superb Mariposa has mostly white petals, with a red blotch surrounded by yellow. Yellow Mariposa, also called Gold Nuggetts, has yellow petals often with a red or brown blotch. The hybrids (shown here) have many combinations of these colors.
Blooms Late April to early June.

CREAM CUPS

Platystemon californicus
Family Poppy

This plant has smaller flowers than the related California Poppy, usually with six petals instead of four. It prefers short grassland, and forms large patches of pale cream which stand out among carpets of other colors in the big meadows. The buds are nodding, and the stems are covered with bristly hairs. Often, two shades of yellow can be seen in each petal.
Blooms Late March to April

Richards Lyon

John Game

TIDY TIPS

Layia chrysanthemoides
Family Sunflower

Two kinds of Tidy Tips grow in Bear Valley, and are major contributors to the huge carpets of yellow seen here in April. One kind has white tips to the outer petals, which give this plant its name. The other kind (below) has solid yellow petals. However, the kind with solid yellow petals in Bear Valley usually has white tips to the petals elsewhere in California, and is the common 'Tidy Tips' species nearer the coast.

Blooms Mid-April to early May

YELLOW TIDY TIPS

Layia platyglossa
Family Sunflower

The two kinds of Tidy Tips in Bear Valley (see above) also differ in the shape of the green flaps (known as "bracts") on the underside of each flower head. This difference applies everywhere, whereas the color difference depends on location. The bracts are much shorter in *L. platyglossa* than they are in *L. chrysanthemoides*. It has been said that in some years an ant could walk across the Bear Valley meadows on the petals of Tidy Tips, never touching the ground.

CUPPED MONOLOPIA
Monolopia major
Family Sunflower

This is another plant with yellow daisy-like flowers, taller than Tidy Tips or Goldfields. The leaves are covered with flattened hairs to give a silky appearance. The bracts, which are the green parts behind the flower heads, are joined into a cup, edged with large teeth. The outer petals, or "rays", are broad with squarish ends. This plant can be seen on the west side of the road near the north end of the Bear Valley flower meadows.
Blooms April to May

GOLDFIELDS
Lasthenia californica
Family Sunflower

This plant is widespread in California and carpets grasslands in such numbers that it turns the open meadows golden, as its name implies. The yellow daisy-like flower heads are smaller than those of Tidy Tips, and are typically an inch in diameter. The narrow leaves are in opposite pairs on the stem. Two very similar species occur in the valley. California Goldfields is pictured. Yellow-rayed Goldfields is taller and prefers damper soil.
Blooms March to May

BALSAMROOT
Balsamorhiza macrolepis
Family Sunflower

This plant is uncommon, but its striking yellow flowers can be seen from the road near the north end of Walker Ridge. It is related to Mule Ears, but is easily distinguished from it and other similar species in the area by the leaves. These leaves are divided into many segments, and have an almost fern-like appearance. The plants are perennial and grow from fleshy taproots. The flower heads are borne singly on long stems.

Blooms April to May.

WOOLLY SUNFLOWER
Eriophyllum lanatum var. achillaeoides
Family Sunflower

This is common in dry sunny spots along the sides of Bear Valley but does not grow in the open meadows. It is slightly shrubby, with silvery foliage. The leaves are divided into narrow segments and the golden-yellow flower heads are borne in loose clusters, on long stalks. This plant occurs throughout most of Western America, and has many varieties.

Blooms April to June

Stephen W. Edwards

John Game

YELLOW FAIRY LANTERNS
Calochortus amabilis
Family Lily

Fairy Lanterns are relatives of the Mariposa Lilies. They have nodding flowers with closed petals that form a globe. Yellow Fairy Lanterns are common in the brushy hills of California's North Coast Ranges, and occur on the sides of Bear Valley. The petals are fringed with short, thick hairs. The seeds are borne in nodding capsules with winged edges.
Blooms April to May

MULE EARS
Wyethia glabra
Family Sunflower

This plant gets its name from the shape of the leaves. It grows on grassy banks and is easily recognized by the huge flower heads, which are among the largest of any Californian plant. Each head is made up of many small individual flowers. A closely related species in this area is Narrow-leafed Mule Ears. The central disk part of its flower heads is smaller in proportion to the outer petals, and it has narrower leaves.
Blooms April to June

John Game

Jake Ruygt

DOUGLAS' VIOLET

Viola douglasii
Family Violet

Despite the name, many kinds of Violet are actually yellow or other colors. This species has large yellow flowers on low stems in short grassland. It can be distinguished from similar species in the Bear Valley area by the leaves, which are divided into segments. Brown veins mark the center of the flower, and the upper petals are dark on the back. Douglas' Violet grows on the knoll just south of the large meadows of the valley.
Blooms Late March to May

CANYON DUDLEYA

Dudleya cymosa
Family Stonecrop

This plant occurs on rocky outcrops on the southern part of Bear Valley Road. It has thick fleshy leaves in rosettes close to the ground. The reddish stems emerge from the sides of the rosettes and are topped by clusters of yellow bell-shaped flowers. It grows in full sun, and the succulent leaves aid in storing water extracted by the deep roots.
Blooms April to May

Richards Lyon

Richards Lyon

CALIFORNIA POPPY
Eschscholzia californica
Family Poppy

California's State Flower is well represented in Bear Valley. It is a major contributor to the huge sweeps of color that fill the landscape here in mid-April. The best poppy show is usually in the northern fields. The plants here are unusually large and are a deep shade of orange, contrasting dramatically with the blue Lupines and purple Owl's Clover.

Blooms April and May

DOUGLAS WALLFLOWER
Erysimum capitatum
Family Mustard

This plant has upright stems that can be three feet tall. It grows on the slopes along Bear Valley Road, usually in partial shade. The flowers are a striking orange, and have four petals. The fruits are long narrow pods with four angles. Each plant lives for two years, forming a rosette of leaves the first year followed by a flowering stem the second year. The stem leaves are very narrow and toothed along the edges.

Blooms March to June

Richards Lyon

Richards Lyon

BLUE-EYED GRASS
Sisyrhynchium bellum
Family Iris

This plant is common in some of the damper meadows, especially toward the northern end of Bear Valley. The narrow sword-like leaves are characteristic of the Iris family, although the flowers are much smaller than those of the true Irises. The flower color is variable but is usually a deep blue to purple.
Blooms April and May

BABY BLUE EYES
Nemophila menziesii
Family Waterleaf

This familiar flower is often grown as a garden annual, but it is widespread as a California native in open spots and grassland. The highly attractive flowers range from sky blue to pale blue with whitish centers. It is common in Bear Valley, forming bright, low mats. The leaves are deeply lobed and toothed.
Blooms March to May

John Game

John Game

MINIATURE LUPINE

Lupinus bicolor
Family Pea

More than eighty species of lupine are found in California. Miniature Lupine is one of the most widespread. In many areas, including Bear Valley, it grows in such profusion that despite its small size, great masses of color are formed in open grassland. This species is variable, but the Bear Valley plants are deep to bright blue, with some white markings. In good years, blue Lupines form dramatic color contrasts with nearby carpets of Yellow Layia, Tidy Tips and Poppies.

Blooms April

ROYAL LARKSPUR

Delphinium variegatum
Family Buttercup

Several species of blue larkspur occur in Californian grasslands, but Royal Larkspur is distinguished by extra large flowers with a deep, intense blue color. Fine stands of this plant occur near the knoll at the southern end of the large meadows of Bear Valley. Western Larkspur is a similar species in the valley, with smaller flowers of a paler blue.

Blooms April

VALLEY DOWNINGIA
Downingia pulchella
Family Bluebell

Two kinds of Downingia occur in Bear Valley. They are low annual plants with distinctive blue flowers like some of the garden Lobelias. Downingias are nearly unique to California, although some also occur in Chile. They need areas that are wet in Spring but dry in Summer. These areas occur on clay soil where shallow pools can form from winter rains. Downingias grow in the northern meadows just west of Bear Valley Road.
Blooms April to early June

COMMON BLUE CUP
Githopsis specularioides
Family Bluebell

In addition to the large showy flowers that make up the big sweeps of color in Bear Valley, a great variety of smaller species occur here, adding diversity and eliciting more careful attention. Common Blue Cup is easily overlooked, but replicates the beauty of many larger flowers on a miniature scale. This photograph was taken on the knoll at the south end of the large meadows. The plant is about one inch tall.
Blooms April to May

Richards Lyon

John Game

CHINESE HOUSES
Collinsia heterophylla
Family Snapdragon

This is a common Californian annual plant of light shade, related to Blue-Eyed Mary. It grows near woods on the drained slopes around Bear Valley. The flowers are in whorls around the upright stem, and are said to resemble a Chinese pagoda. Each flower has a pale upper lip and a much darker lower lip. The lance-shaped leaves are in opposite pairs on the stem, and have toothed edges.
Blooms April to May

BLUE-EYED MARY
Collinsia sparsiflora
Family Snapdragon

This small annual grows both in open woodland and in the short grass of Bear Valley's meadows. The individual flowers have long stalks, and are in opposite pairs instead of the whorls seen in related Chinese Houses. The petals are usually bluish-purple, but this plant is variable with at least two varieties in the area. The narrow leaves are also in opposite pairs.
Blooms March to April

John Game

Richards Lyon

DEER BRUSH

Ceanothus intergerrimus
Family Buckthorn

Many kinds of flowering shrubs and trees occur in the
Bear Valley/Walker Ridge area. Three are presented in
this book. Deer Brush has clusters of many small blue
flowers and deep green oval deciduous leaves. It is also
known as California Lilac. Buckbrush (*Ceanothus
cuneatus*) is a related species in this area with white
flowers and smaller more leathery evergreen leaves. Both
species occur in dry, open or brushy areas.
Blooms May to June.

ITHURIEL'S SPEAR

Triteleia laxa
Family Lily

This plant is widespread in Californian grasslands, and is
one of the State's most distinctive wildflowers. Clusters
of blue to purple funnel-shaped flowers top stems that
can be more than two feet tall. Much shorter forms occur,
especially near the coast. It is common in and near Bear
Valley, but usually grows in small groups rather than broad
sweeps.
Blooms April to May

Richards Lyon

John Game

WILD HYACINTH

Dichelostemma capitatum
Family Lily

This flower (also called "Blue Dicks") is another famous California native, found throughout the state except in the high mountains. It is related to Ithuriel's Spear and several other plants in this area, but can be distinguished by the flowers. These are smaller and much more tightly clustered at the top of the stem. The leaves are very narrow and emerge from the base of the stem. The bulbs are edible but should not be removed from the wild.
Blooms Late March to April

INDIAN PINK

Silene californica
Family Pink

This plant forms low spreading patches in brushy rocky areas and can be seen along Bear Valley Road in the southern narrow section. It is not common here, but the large crimson flowers are conspicuous. The petals are deeply divided into narrow lobes. The leaves are oval and softly hairy, and are placed in pairs on the stem. This plant is related to the Campion or Catchfly flowers.
Blooms   April to May

INDIAN WARRIOR
Pedicularis densiflora
Family Snapdragon

This is one of the first plants to bloom in Spring. It is found in brushy spots along the sides of the Valley, and is partially parasitic, feeding on the roots of shrubs. The dark green leaves are divided into narrow segments and the tubular flowers are in dense spikes. Each flower has a straight beak and a lower lip of three small lobes set well back on the tube.

Blooms February to April

DOUGLAS' MONKEY FLOWER
PURPLE MOUSE EARS
Mimulus douglasii
Family Snapdragon

Several kinds of small red Monkey Flowers occur in this area, usually on bare soil or gravelly areas with some moisture in Spring. They are annuals with tubular flowers typical of the snapdragon family. This species can be distinguished by the wide opening at the front of the throat, which has almost no lower lip, giving it a "chinless" appearance. The flowers are large for the size of the plant, which is usually less than two inches tall.

Blooms April to May

Richards Lyon

John Game

RED MAIDS
Calindrinia ciliata
Family Purslane

This low, sprawling plant is distinguished by the intense red color of the petals. It is common in most of California, and is found in cultivated fields as well as natural sandy or grassy areas. It is one of the first flowers to bloom in Spring in Bear Valley, and can be seen with the Adobe Lilies. Here, its flowers are often flat on the ground, but face straight upwards.
Blooms February to April

SICKLE-LEAFED ONION
Allium falcifolium
Family Lily

More than thirty kinds of Onion occur in California, and at least five are in the Bear Valley/Walker Ridge area. This species resembles Crater Onion in having flower-heads that are close to the ground. Typically the flowers are much darker purple, although some plants have white flowers. Also, the petals are longer and narrower and the leaves are flattened in a different way and curved like a sickle. This plant grows on rocky serpentine soils especially on Walker Ridge.
Blooms March to April

Stephen W. Edwards

John Game

PURDY'S FRINGED ONION
Allium fimbriatum var. purdyi
Family Lily

This is a rare variety of onion that grows on rocky slopes near the southern entrance of Bear Valley. The leaves are very narrow and cylindrical in cross-section. Like many of the unusual plants in the area, this species thrives in areas influenced by the mineral serpentinite. This creates soils which are toxic to many common plant species, leaving the rarer ones to survive with less competition.
Blooms April to May

CRATER ONION
Allium cratericola
Family Lily

This unusual onion gets its name from a preference for the cindery soils of old volcanic craters. It is also found in areas influenced by serpentine, including the gravelly serpentine soils of Walker Ridge. The pale pink flowers are tightly clustered and form a ball which sits very close to the ground, since the stalk is short and partly buried. Each bulb also sends up one or two long strap-shaped leaves in early Spring.
Blooms April to May

Richards Lyon

John Game

HENDERSON'S SHOOTING STAR
Dodecatheon herdersonii
Family Primrose

This attractive plant is about a foot tall and often grows in large but open patches on grassy slopes or chaparral. It is one of the first flowers to bloom in early Spring. The oval leaves form a rosette at the base of the upright stems. It is closely related to the cyclamens that are grown in horticulture. This can be seen from the unusual flowers, which point downwards with the petals folded backwards.
Blooms February to May.

REDBUD
Cercis occidentalis
Family Senna

This shrub or small tree is scattered along Bear Valley Road and is common on dry slopes and canyons. It can also grow near stream banks, but is usually set back from the water. Its numerous dramatic purple flowers are one of the first signs that Winter is ending in Northern California. The roundish leaves come out after the flowers, and the seeds are formed in conspicuous oblong pods.
Blooms March

John Game

John Game

ADOBE LILY
Fritillaria pluriflora
Family Lily

This is the most famous plant of Bear Valley. In a good year, many thousands of these lilies bloom in a huge sweep in fields west of the road. Smaller groups occur elsewhere in the Valley. The long-lived bulbs are deeply buried in the clay soil and go dormant in early Summer until the next rains. This is a rare plant of inland valleys in Northern California. The population in Bear Valley is by far the largest, and may contain more plants than all the others combined. Conserving this historic population is a key objective for the future of the valley.

Blooms Mid to late March.

LARGE FLOWERED STAR TULIP
Calochortus uniflorus
Family Lily

This is a low growing plant which thrives on damp soil. It can be seen alongside Bear Valley Road in the short section that runs east to west through the meadows shortly before the road turns north again. It occurs in some of the damper fields and alongside the creeks. It is related to Mariposa Lilies and Fairy Lanterns.

Blooms April to May

John Game

John Game

JEPSON'S MILKVETCH

Astragalus rattanii var. jepsonianus

Family Pea

Many species of Milkvetch occur in California. They are related to Peas and true Vetches. This rare variety is found only in Colusa and nearby counties. It grows on grassy hillsides influenced by serpentine soil. The leaves are divided into separate leaflets, with one leaflet at the end. The flowers are borne in a cluster at the end of the stem. Each flower is purple and white, giving distinction to this small annual.

Blooms April to June

FAREWELL TO SPRING
TRACY'S CLARKIA

Clarkia gracilis ssp. tracyi

Family Evening Primrose

The crowded flowers of this plant form dense patches of pink at spots along the southern, rocky part of Bear Valley Road. Like other members of this family, they have four petals. This is a rare variety of Slender Clarkia, with larger petals than usual for this species. Several related forms of Clarkia with smaller petals occur in the valley.

Blooms May to June

John Game

Stephen W. Edwards

BITTERROOT
Lewisia rediviva
Family Purslane

This plant is easy to recognize from the large rose-pink flowers that lie close to the ground. The leaves are in rosettes below the flowers, and are very narrow but fleshy. There is a deep tap root below each rosette, which enables the plant to thrive in dry places. Bitteroot grows in open rocky habitats, and here is found on the serpentine of Walker Ridge and elsewhere. It is perennial, but goes dormant from late Summer to early Spring.
Blooms April to May

SPLENDID MARIPOSA LILY
Calochortus splendens
Family Lily

This tall Mariposa Lily has flowers that are solid pink to lavender, sometimes with a darker zone at the base of the petals. It grows near the road in the southern part of Bear Valley, and on nearby Walker Ridge. It is usually found further south in California. Some of the plants on Walker Ridge are an unusual bright pink color. However, the typical lavender form occurs in the valley.
Blooms May to June

Jake Ruygt

John Game

PURPLE OWL'S CLOVER
Castilleja exserta
Family Snapdragon

This plant adds a shade of purple to the Spring color
display. It grows in separate clumps among the other
flowers, and is widespread in the meadows. It is related
to Indian Paintbrush and Butter-and-Eggs. Each flower
has three small sacs and a hooked beak with dense hairs.
These hairs help distinguish this species from other kinds
of Owl's Clover in the valley.
Blooms April

BIRD'S EYE GILIA
Gilia tricolor ssp. tricolor
Family Phlox

At least ten kinds of wildflower in the Phlox family occur
in the Bear Valley area, and some are common in the
grassy meadows. Bird's Eye Gilia is one of the prettiest.
The multiple shades of color in the flowers are offset by
bright green leaves divided into narrow lobes. The tube
below the five petals is usually yellow and the stamens
are blue. This annual is common in short grassland but
does not compete with dense vegetation.
Blooms March to May

John Game

John Game

PURDY'S FRITILLARY
Fritillaria purdyi
Family Lily

This is related to the Adobe Lily, but grows in the drained rocky soils of nearby slopes and ridges instead of the open meadows. The flowers are brownish and mottled and can be upright or drooping. Two more species of Fritillary occur in this area. They are much taller and have narrow leaves around an upright stem. Checker Lily (*F. affinis*) has greenish mottled flowers, whereas Scarlet Fritillary (*F. recurva*) is deep red.
Blooms March to April

STREAM ORCHID
Epipactis gigantea
Family Orchid

Stream Orchid occurs in just a few places along streams in the hills above Bear Valley. It is a striking plant with spikes of complex greenish brown flowers. Each flower has a lower lip with red or purple markings. The leaves have parallel veins and are arranged alternately on the stem. The plants are perennial and spread from a creeping rootstock, but the spikes die back each year in the Fall.
Blooms May to early June

Latin and English Index